# How To...

BY DAVID LEWITT

# PLAY ROCK DRUMS

T0085316

To access audio visit:
**www.halleonard.com/mylibrary**

Enter Code
5130-7892-5101-1967

ISBN 978-1-4950-0317-2

## HAL•LEONARD® CORPORATION

7777 W. BLUEMOUND RD. P.O. BOX 13819 MILWAUKEE, WI 53213

Copyright © 2015 by HAL LEONARD CORPORATION
International Copyright Secured   All Rights Reserved

In Australia Contact:
**Hal Leonard Australia Pty. Ltd.**
4 Lentara Court
Cheltenham, Victoria, 3192 Australia
Email: ausadmin@halleonard.com.au

No part of this publication may be reproduced in any form or by
any means without the prior written permission of the Publisher.

Visit Hal Leonard Online at
**www.halleonard.com**

# CONTENTS

# INTRODUCTION

In rock and roll music, drummers play the key role in directing and steering the band through a song. They provide the foundation upon which the rest of the music and musicians build upon. Metaphorically speaking, you could describe the drummer as a building's foundation. If music is a basketball team, the drummer is the point guard—he or she calls the play (the count off) and sets it up for the rest of the team (the band). If you need yet another analogy, you could call the drummer a bus driver—the person who controls the vehicle (the band) and safely brings the passengers to their destination. Suffice it to say that no building can stand without a solid foundation, no basketball team can play and win without a great point guard, and no bus will get anywhere safely without a skilled driver.

All that being said, a drummer basically performs two main tasks in rock music: playing beats and playing fills. If you can perform a solid repertoire of beats and fills well, then you can play drums for a rock band. So let's learn how to play some rock 'n' roll drums!

## AUDIO

There are audio files for each example so you can hear what the material should sound like. To access all of the audio examples that accompany this book, simply go to www.halleonard.com/mylibarary and enter the code found on page 1.

# DRUM KEY

| Crash | Closed Hi-Hat | Open Hi-Hat | Ride Cymbal | Bell of Ride | Tom 1 | Tom 2 | Snare Drum | Floor Tom | Bass Drum | Stick Click |

# ROCK DRUMMING THEORY

Think about your favorite rock song. Now think about the beat the drummer is playing for that song. What are the common elements in most, if not nearly **all**, of the beats that you hear in rock music? Well, there are four of them:

1. The beat is nearly always in 4/4, so we count: 1 + 2 + 3 + 4 + ("one and two and three and four and").

2. The bass drum is on the "1," or the *downbeat*, of the groove (and quite often on beat 3 as well, but not always).

3. The snare plays on the "2" and the "4" counts of the measure.

4. There's a steady rhythm played on the hi-hat or ride cymbal; it's most often eighth notes, but it can sometimes be quarter notes or 16th notes.

Think about it for a second; what rock song doesn't have these four things? Let's think of some of the most popular songs in rock music—the classics. A great one that comes to mind is "Brown Sugar" by the Rolling Stones: the bass drum is on beat 1 (and 3 in this case, as in many others), the snare is on beats 2 and 4, and the hi-hat is playing eighth notes. How about "I Wanna Hold Your Hand" by the Beatles? Same thing: bass drum on the downbeat (and beat 3), snare on 2 and 4, and the hi-hat playing eighth notes. "Rock and Roll" by Led Zeppelin? After the opening lead-in intro fill (probably the most "classic" of all rock intro fills), it's the same as the others.

What about the Who and one of their biggest hits: "Who Are You?" After the intro section (where the drummer is playing 16th notes on the hi-hat along with the opening guitar and keyboard riff), the beat once again settles into bass drum on 1 (and 3), snare on 2 and 4 (in this case, also with crash cymbals backing up the snare), and the hi-hat playing eighth notes. Bruce Springsteen's "Born in the USA"—same deal. "Billie Jean" by Michael Jackson? Check! "Dancing in the Dark" by Bruce Springsteen? Check! "Back in Black" by AC/DC? "The Joker" by the Steve Miller Band? What about Elton John's "Crocodile Rock"? Same! The list goes on and on. How about "Maggie May" and "You Wear It Well" by Rod Stewart? Both of these songs have all the elements described above but with quarter notes on the hi-hat.

So let's get to it and start learning the "meat and potatoes" of rock drumming: the *beats* and the *fills*. 1, 2, ready, and go!

**Note:** Although all the beats written in this book are written for the hi-hat, please remember that any of them can be played on the ride cymbal as well.

# EIGHTH-NOTE CLASSIC ROCK BEATS

This one is referred to as "four on the floor" due to the bass drum playing on all four beats of the measure.

*(1st time only)*

The rest of these beats follow the ideas talked about in the intro: the bass drum is on beat 1, the snare is on beats 2 and 4. The bass drum will also appear on beat 3 for the next several beats.

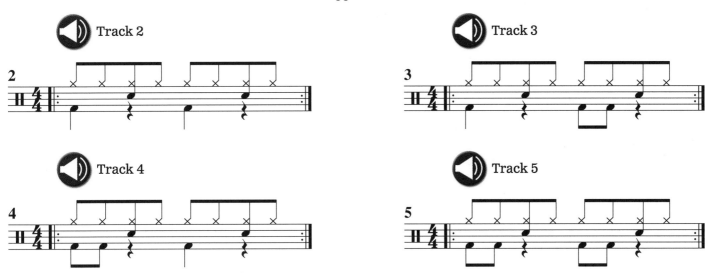

This is a great groove used both in rock and R&B. It contains the "four on the floor" bass drum pattern with an extra note on the "and" of beat 3.

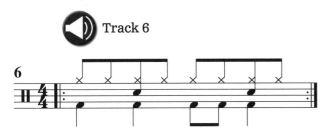

Now the bass drum will start to incorporate variations on the "and" of beat 2.

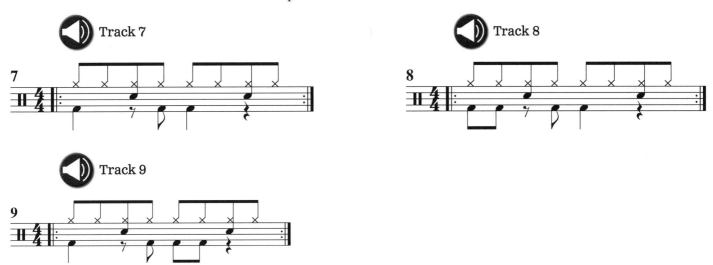

Now let's add the "and" of beat 4. I call this the "rock bossa" because of the bossa nova bass drum pattern.

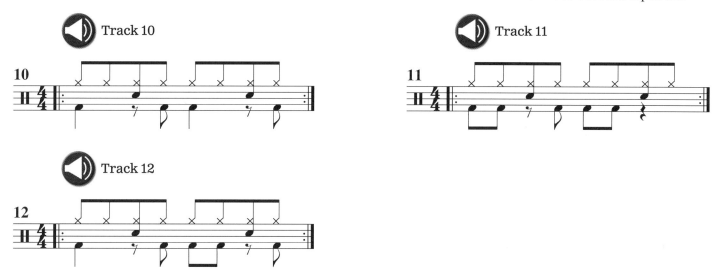

**Track 10**

**Track 11**

**Track 12**

I call this next one the "train beat" because of the repetitive nature of the groove, which sounds like a train locomotive.

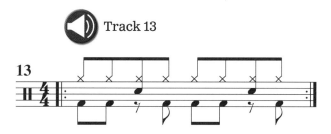

**Track 13**

Now we'll start syncopating around beat 3 in the bass drum.

**Track 14**

**Track 15**

**Track 16**

**Track 17**

Now let's add the "and" of beat 4 in the bass drum to create a very propulsive and forward-moving groove.

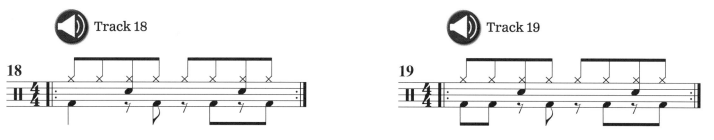

**Track 18**

**Track 19**

We can also leave more space in the beat by putting the bass drum on the "and" of beat 3. Remember that we always have the downbeats, or the "1" count, on the bass drum.

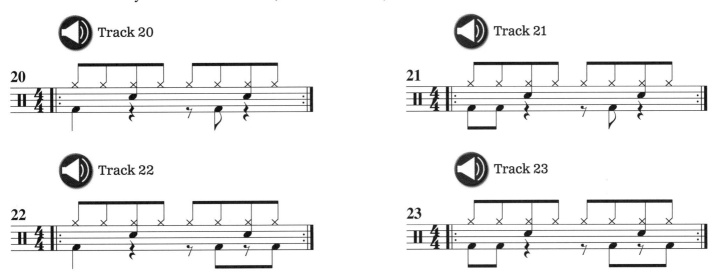

Although many songs use one-bar patterns as the primary beat of a song, often a two-bar pattern—combining two different beats—will be used. Here are some two-bar grooves that you will find useful.

Track 29

Track 30

Track 31

Track 32

# DRUM FILL THEORY

The purpose of a drum fill in any form of music—and particularly in rock music—is to steer or otherwise set up the next phrase or section of the piece. It's the drummer's way of telling the band and the listener that something new—be it the next verse or chorus, or perhaps a solo or instrumental section—is coming soon.

In rock music, there are some basic "rules" that are, for the most part, adhered to by the drummer. The first "rule" is that the fill will move from one of two drums—either the snare or the highest or second highest tom—and descend down the toms from there. Typically a rock drum fill will start on the snare and use all three toms in a descending order. (For the purpose of this book, we are using the standard set-up of two rack toms and one floor tom.) This is not to say that all fills do this (or must do this), but rather that most of the time this is how it's done by drummers in the context of rock music. It is rare, though it does happen, that drum fills deviate from this "high-to-low" concept.

Another thing to remember is that the fill usually matches the "feel" of the beat you're playing; in other words, if your beat is in an eighth-note feel, your fill will have an eighth- or 16th-note feel to it. Generally speaking, the rhythm you're playing on the hi-hat or ride cymbal will dictate what kind of fill will work. If it's a triplet feel like, say, the rock shuffle, your fill will use a triplet feel or rhythm. If it's an eighth-note feel, such as the "classic" beats in the first chapter or the 12/8 beats, your fill will match the eighth-note feel of the ride or hi-hat cymbal pattern and can utilize eighth and 16th notes. This will provide an even flow musically from the beat into the fill and back to the beat again. Lastly, the fill will usually end with a combination of the crash cymbal and the bass drum on beat 1 of the next measure.

If you follow these "rules," you will be the kind of drummer that other musicians—particularly bass players—will love to play with.

# EIGHTH-NOTE CLASSIC ROCK BEATS WITH FILLS

Practice these fills using the following routine: three bars of the groove (you can use any of the one-bar classic eighth-note grooves), and then one bar of the fill. For the following "fill" section, we'll use Beat #3 from the Eighth-Note Classic Rock Beats chapter as our foundation beat.

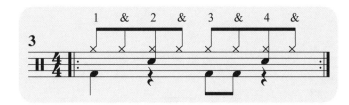

We call this the "four-bar phrase with a fill" concept. In this book, end the fill on the downbeat of the following measure with the bass drum and crash cymbal. You can link these phrases together by continuing to the next four-bar phrase. We'll keep the bass drum on quarter notes for all the fills in this section.

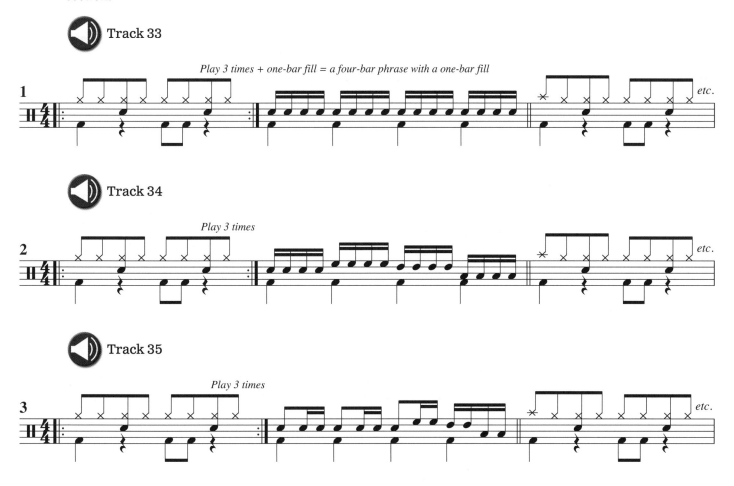

Track 33

Track 34

Track 35

**Track 36**

**Track 37**

**Track 38**

**Track 39**

**Track 40**

**Track 41**

 Track 42

## Shorter Fills

While often drum fills occupy one full bar, many times the task of transitioning the music from one section to the next, or denoting the end of a musical phrase, can be done using shorter fills. Here are some examples of one-, two-, and three-beat fills. We'll use the same idea of the "four-bar phrase with a fill" for these examples.

### One-Beat Fills

 Track 43

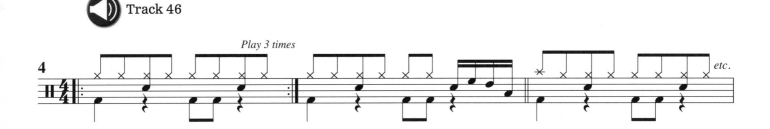

These same fills can be orchestrated using the toms in addition to the snare.

Track 46

Track 47

Track 48

Experiment with your own ideas on how to orchestrate these rhythms as fills. Remember always to end the fills on the downbeat of the following measure with the bass drum and crash cymbal.

## Two-Beat Fills

Now let's check out some two-beat fills. We'll add the bass drum on quarter notes for the fill measures.

Track 49

Track 50

Track 51

Now we can take these same fills that were played on the snare and orchestrate them using the toms and snare.

**Track 52**

**Track 53**

**Track 54**

## Three-Beat Fills

We'll have the bass drum play quarter notes for these fills and orchestrate them around the kit.

**Track 55**

**Track 56**

**Track 57**

*Play 3 times*

Track 59

*Play 3 times*

Track 60

*Play 3 times*

# QUARTER-NOTE CLASSIC ROCK BEATS

Now we'll explore some classic patterns with the hi-hat playing quarter notes. You'll see that most of the following bass and snare patterns are the same as the classic beats with eighth notes in the hi-hat. DO NOT BE FOOLED! Although these grooves may have similar (or identical) snare and bass rhythms, they feel, sound, and are (in my opinion) harder to play because the hi-hat hand (right hand for righties, left hand for lefties) is not playing steady eighth notes. Be sure when playing these beats that the hi-hat is steady and even and that your bass and snare are perfectly placed. Play these beats at around 130 bpm.

Track 61                    Track 62

Track 63                    Track 64

Track 65                    Track 66

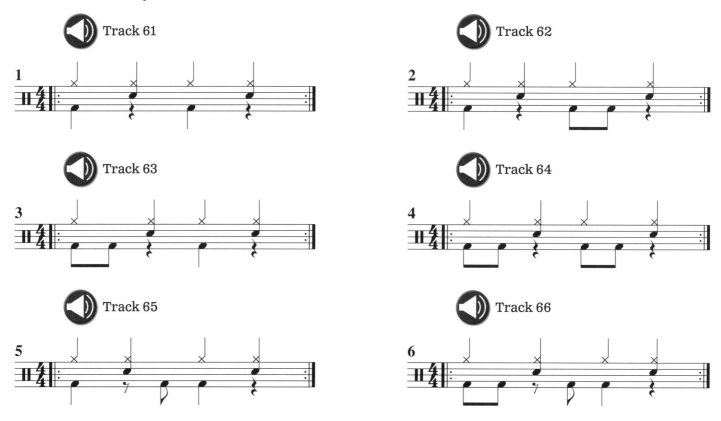

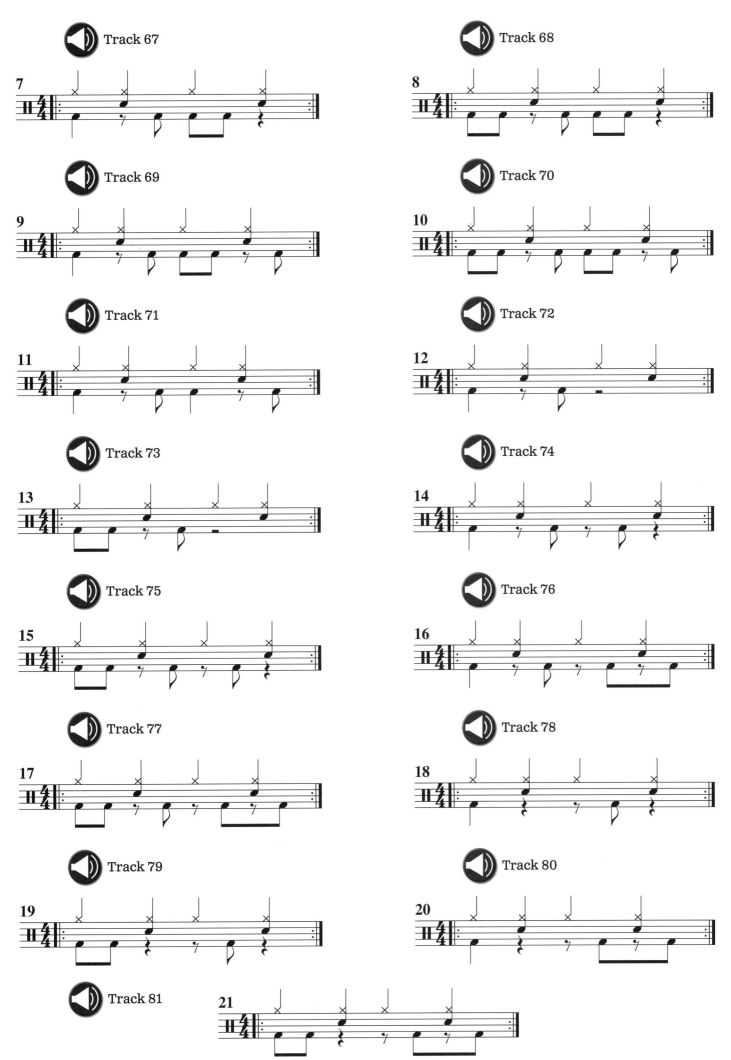

As with the classic eighth-note grooves, quarter-note hi-hat beats are often combined into two-bar patterns. Here are some common two-bar patterns using quarter-note patterns on the hi-hat. Play these beats at a moderate speed of around 110–130 bpm.

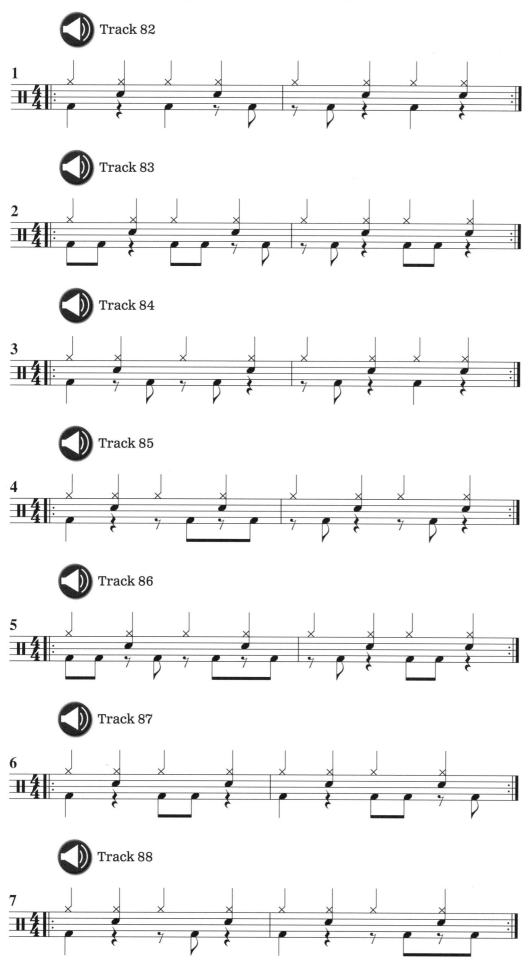

Track 82

Track 83

Track 84

Track 85

Track 86

Track 87

Track 88

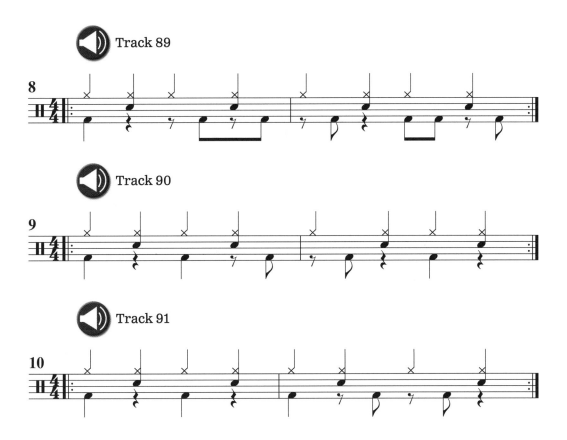

Track 89

Track 90

Track 91

# QUARTER-NOTE CLASSIC ROCK BEATS WITH FILLS

For this section, we'll again use the "four-bar phrase with a fill" concept, meaning that we'll first play three bars of the beat and then one bar of a fill. We'll use Beat #14 from the one-bar beats in the previous chapter. Remember always to end the fill on the downbeat of the following measure with the bass drum and crash cymbal.

## One-Bar Fills

Track 92

Track 93

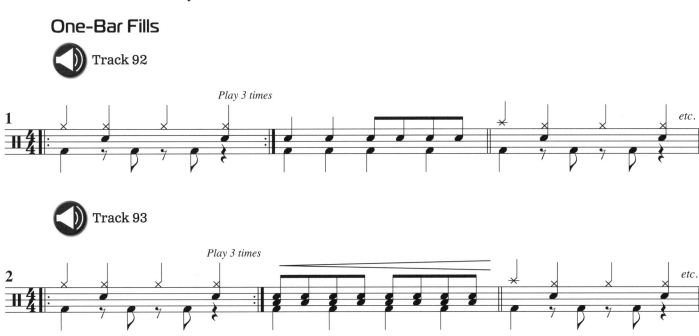

**Track 94**

**Track 95**

## Three-Beat Fills

**Track 97**

**Track 98**

**Track 99**

## Two-Beat Fills

**Track 106**

**Track 107**

**Track 108**

## One-Beat Fills

As mentioned before, a fill can be as short as one beat and still be effective. Here are some examples of one-beat fills in the context of beats that have a quarter-note hi-hat pattern. Again, always end the fill on the downbeat of the next phrase with a crash cymbal and bass drum.

**Track 109**

**Track 110**

**Track 111**

🔊 **Track 112**

# FUNKY ROCK BEATS WITH EIGHTH NOTES ON THE HI-HAT

Now we'll play beats that have some 16th-note syncopation in the snare part. We'll use an eighth-note pattern on the hi-hat. These will be one-bar patterns.

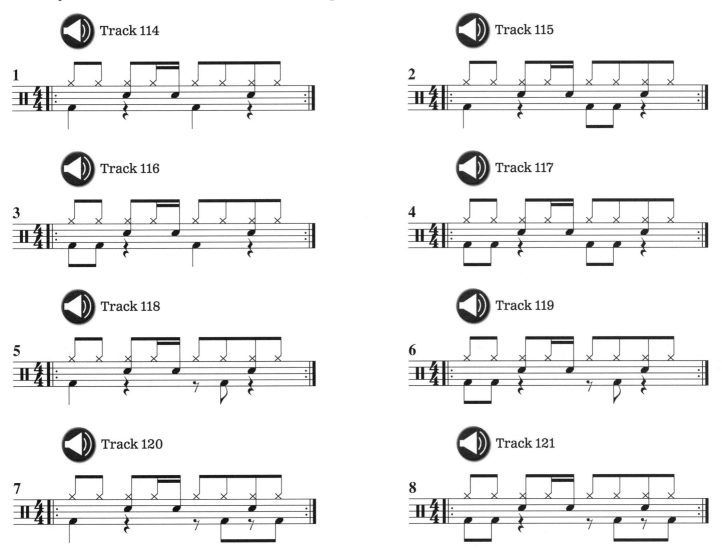

Now let's combine these beats into some cool two-bar patterns. For added color, we'll add the open hi-hat on the "and" of beat 4 in the second bar of the pattern.

## FUNKY ROCK BEATS WITH SYNCOPATION IN THE BASS DRUM

Now we'll add some 16th-note syncopation in the bass drum part.

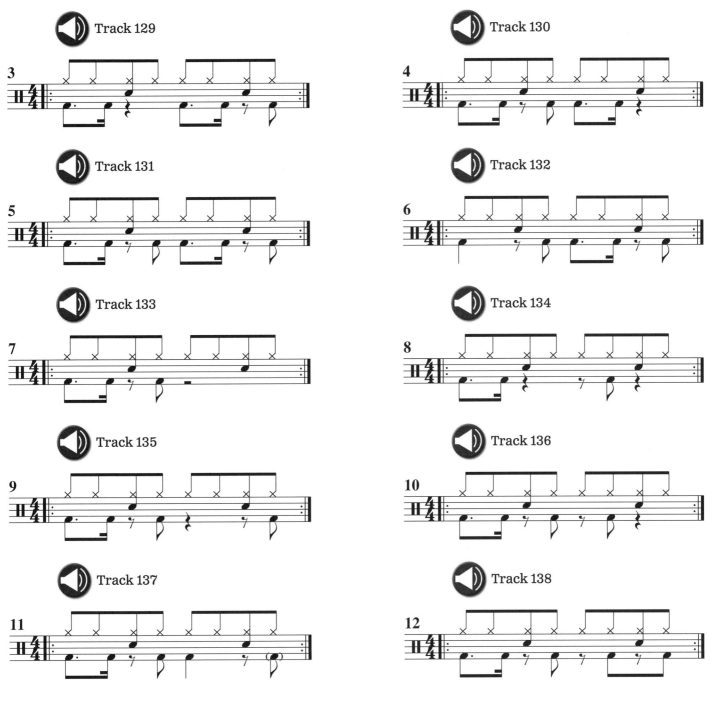

Now we'll bring in some open hi-hat notes to add a bit of color and phrasing to these ideas.

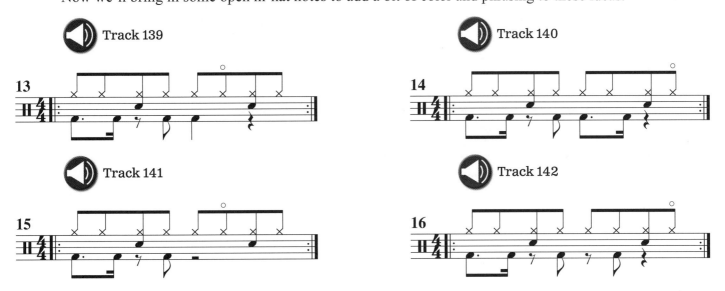

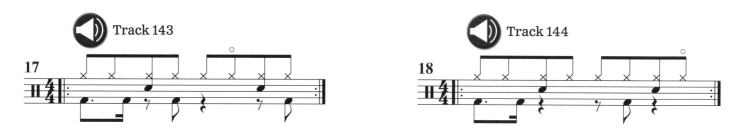

## *Funky Rock Beats in Two-Bar Phrases*

Now let's put all these elements together in some cool two-bar patterns, utilizing syncopated bass drum rhythms and the open hi-hat sound.

# FUNKY ROCK BEATS WITH FILLS

Now we'll explore some one-bar fills for use with funky rock beats. We'll use Beat #5 from the first section of the Funky Rock Beats with Eighth Notes on the Hi-Hat chapter. For this section, we'll have the bass drum play quarter notes for the fill bar. And remember: do I have to say it? Always end the fill on the downbeat of the following phrase with the bass drum and crash cymbal!

## One-Bar Fills

In example #6, notice that the bass drum is incorporated into the fill.

## Three-Beat Fills

For this section, we'll use Beat #10 from the Funky Rock Beats with Syncopation in the Bass Drum chapter. The bass drum part will have some variations added as part of the fill bars.

## Two-Beat Fills

All the same ideas apply here. The bass drum will be more active in these fills.

## One-Beat Fills

You know the drill by now. These fills are really just minor variations of the beat. Keep the momentum going and place all notes precisely. The first three of these are on snare drum only.

 Track 169

 Track 170

Now we'll take those same three fills and use the toms as well.

Track 172

Track 173

Track 174

# ROCK SHUFFLE BEATS

The rock shuffle beat, as opposed to a blues shuffle, is an easy groove to play. In a blues shuffle, the cymbal or hi-hat hand is playing the full "shuffle feel," which is:

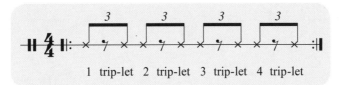

This can be a technically challenging rhythm to play—especially for a long time. However, in a rock shuffle beat, the hi-hat or cymbal pattern is simplified to quarter notes, and the triplet (or "shuffle") feel is implied through the placement of the bass and snare notes. The first shuffle beat you'll play will sound like Beat #1 from the Quarter-Note Classic Rock Beats chapter. Remember that you are always thinking (and feeling) the triplet shuffle feel, which is:

1 trip - let   2 trip - let   3 trip - let   4 trip - let

Track 175                    Track 176

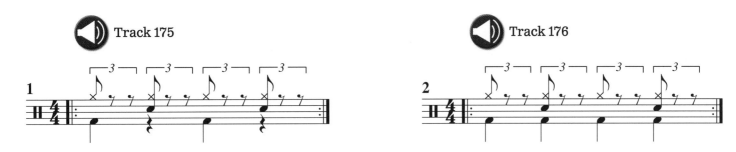

From this point forward, triplets will be indicated on the subdivided parts of the beat.

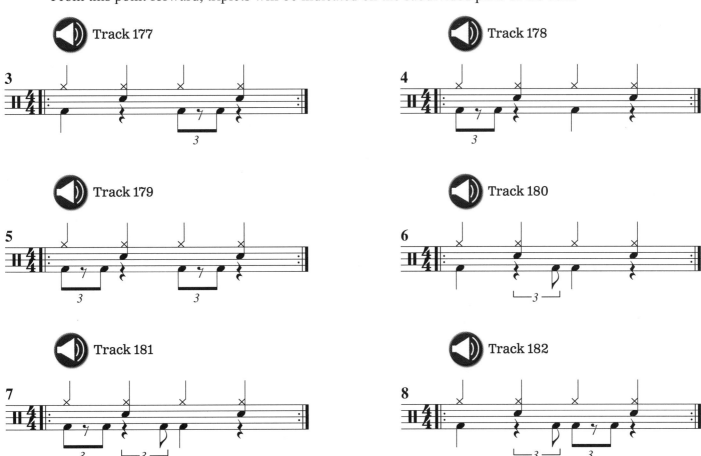

As with all the previous styles of beats, rock shuffle beats can be combined into two-bar phrases as well. Here are some common grooves you'll find useful. Remember: always subdivide triplets when counting and playing these beats.

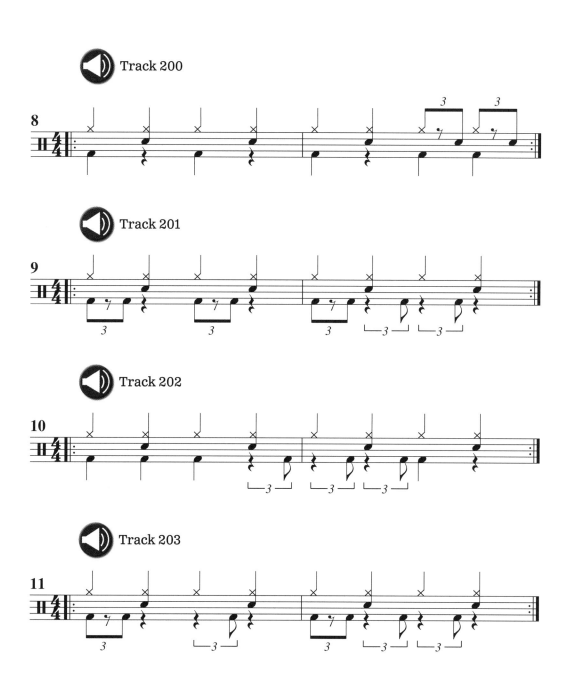

**Track 200**

**8**

**Track 201**

**9**

**Track 202**

**10**

**Track 203**

**11**

# ROCK SHUFFLE BEATS WITH FILLS

Now let's check out some fills for the rock shuffle beat. We'll use Beat #3 from the Rock Shuffle Beats chapter as our base. For these exercises, keep the bass drum in quarter notes for all the fills.

## One-Bar Fills

Track 204

Track 205

Track 206

Track 207

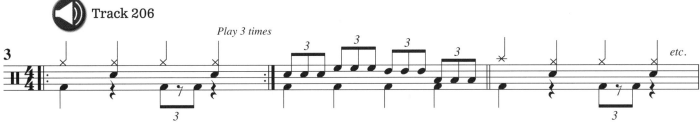

Track 208

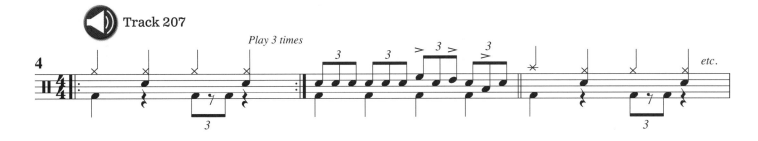

Track 209

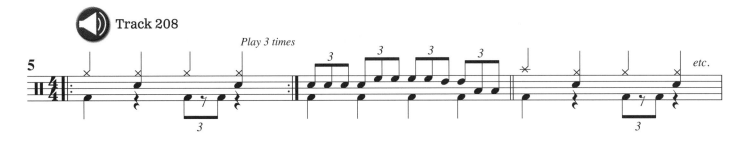

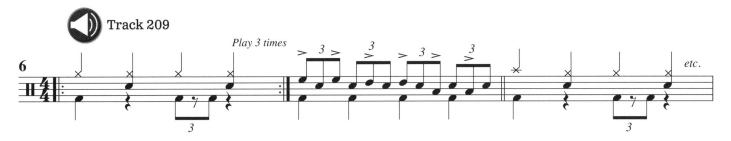

## Three-Beat Fills

Again, the bass drum will be played in quarter notes for the fills.

🔊 Track 210

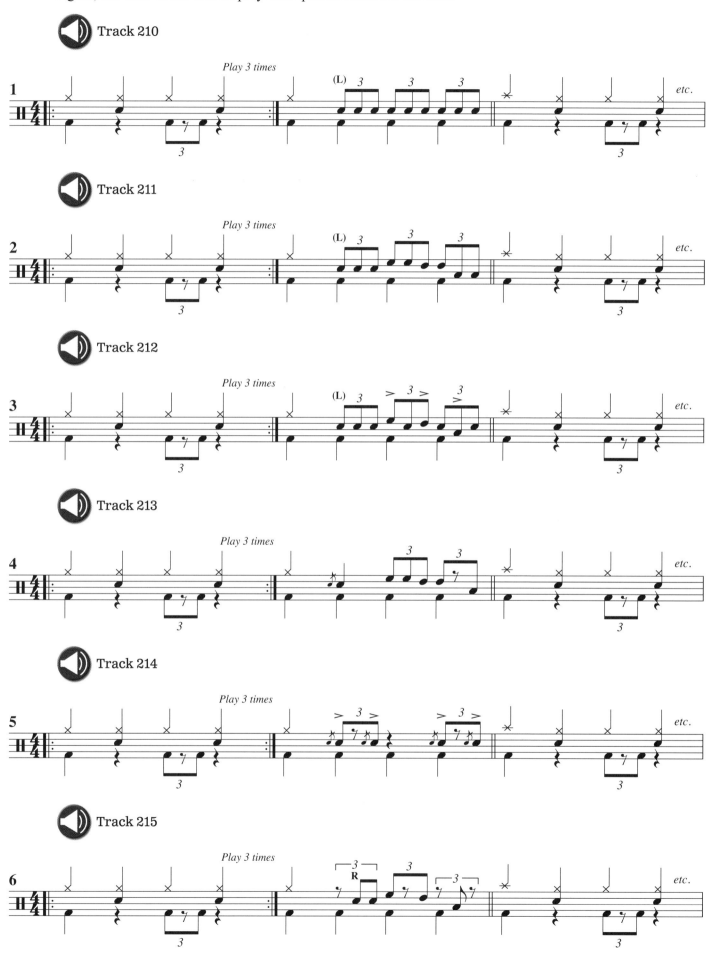

🔊 Track 211

🔊 Track 212

🔊 Track 213

🔊 Track 214

🔊 Track 215

## Two-Beat Fills

## One-Beat Fills

Another beat you hear in rock and blues music is the 12/8 groove. We'll count this beat in four triplet groupings as follows:

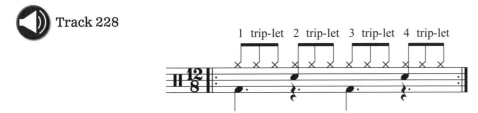

Track 228

Although the measure has twelve eighth notes as the underlying subdivision, rather than counting from one to twelve, we simply divide the beat into four triplets and count it as such.

Here are some 12/8 beats that will be useful:

# 12/8 BEATS WITH FILLS

12/8 beats have a nice rolling kind of feel. Now let's check out some fills for those rolling beats. Once again we'll use the "four-bar phrase with a fill" concept. Beat #8 from the previous chapter will serve as our primary beat.

## One-Bar Fills

## Three-Beat Fills

Track 244

Track 245

Track 246

Track 247

Track 248

Track 249

## Two-Beat Fills

**Track 250**

**1**

**Track 251**

**2**

**Track 252**

**3**

**Track 253**

**4**

**Track 254**

**5**

**Track 255**

**6**

## One-Beat Fills

 Track 256

Track 257

Track 258

Track 259

Track 260

Track 261

# HALF TIME BEATS

Another groove found often in rock music is the half time beat. *Half time* refers to the 4/4 bar being divided in half, with the bass drum sounding on the "1" count and the snare drum sounding on the "3" count.

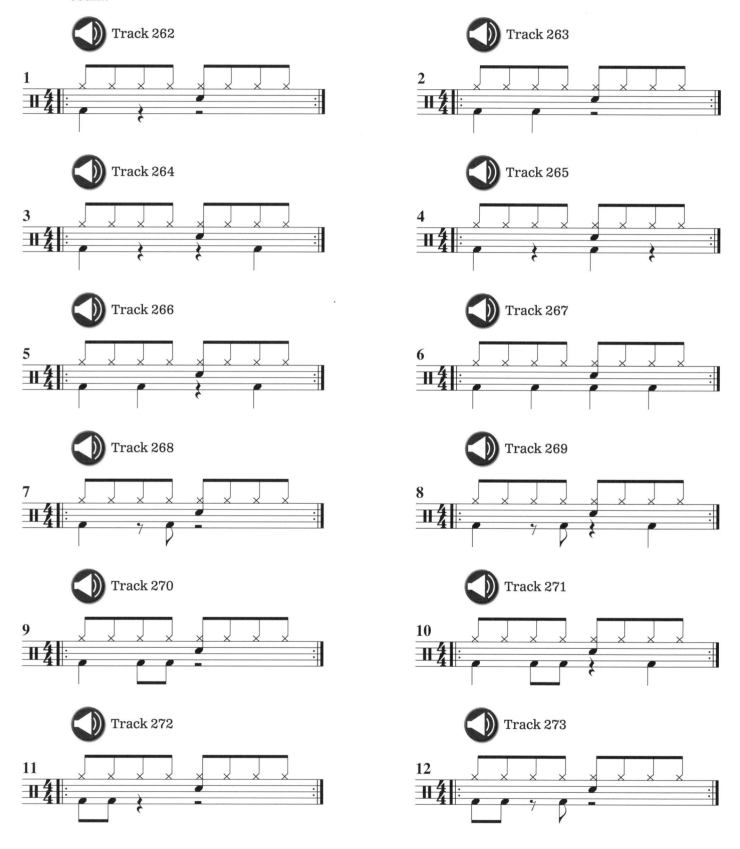

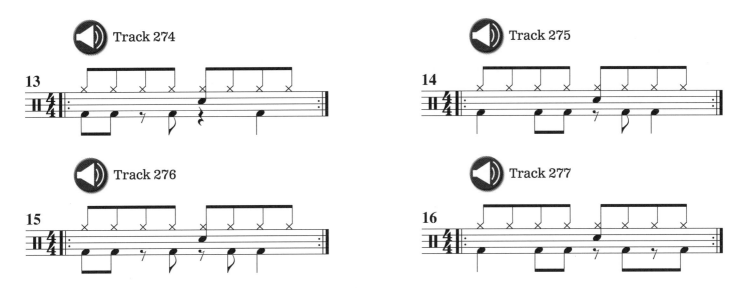

As with all the previous grooves in the book, half time beats can be combined into two-bar phrases. Here are some two-bar half time beats you'll find useful.

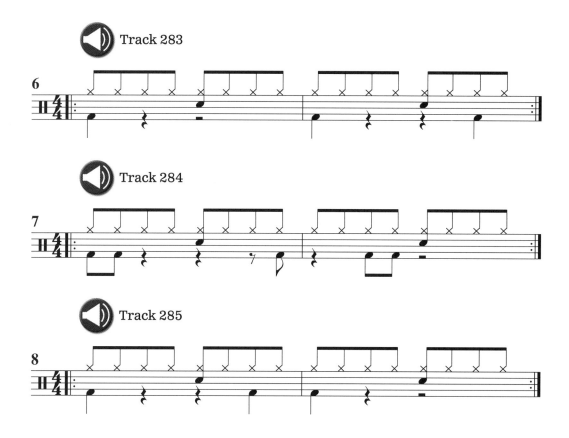

Track 283

Track 284

Track 285

# HALF TIME BEATS WITH FILLS

As before, we'll use the "four-bar phrase with a fill" for these half time beat fills. The bass drum will play on beats 1 and 3 of the fill bar.

## One-Bar Fills

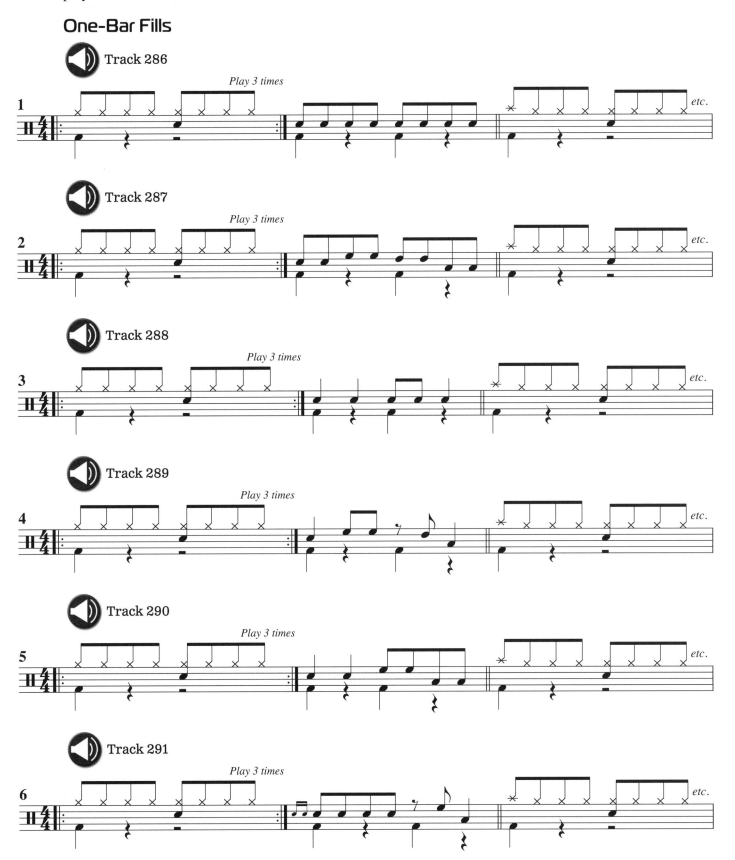

Track 286

Track 287

Track 288

Track 289

Track 290

Track 291

## Three-Beat Fills

Track 292

Track 293

Track 294

Track 295

Track 296

Track 297

## Two-Beat Fills

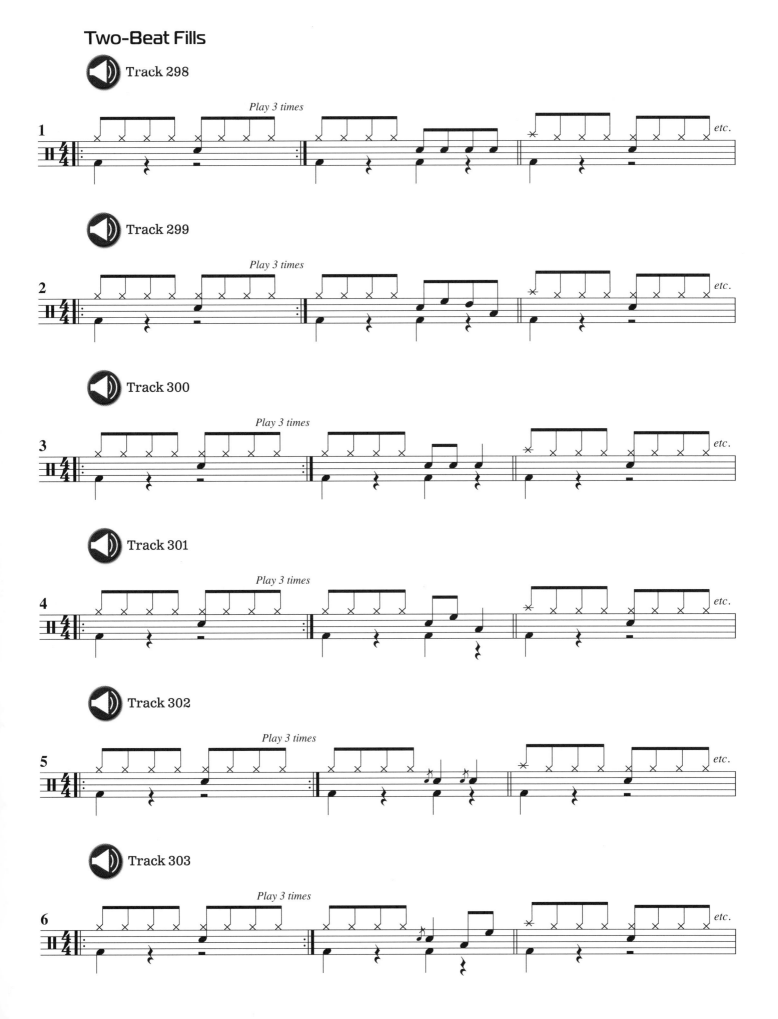

## One-Beat Fills

Track 304

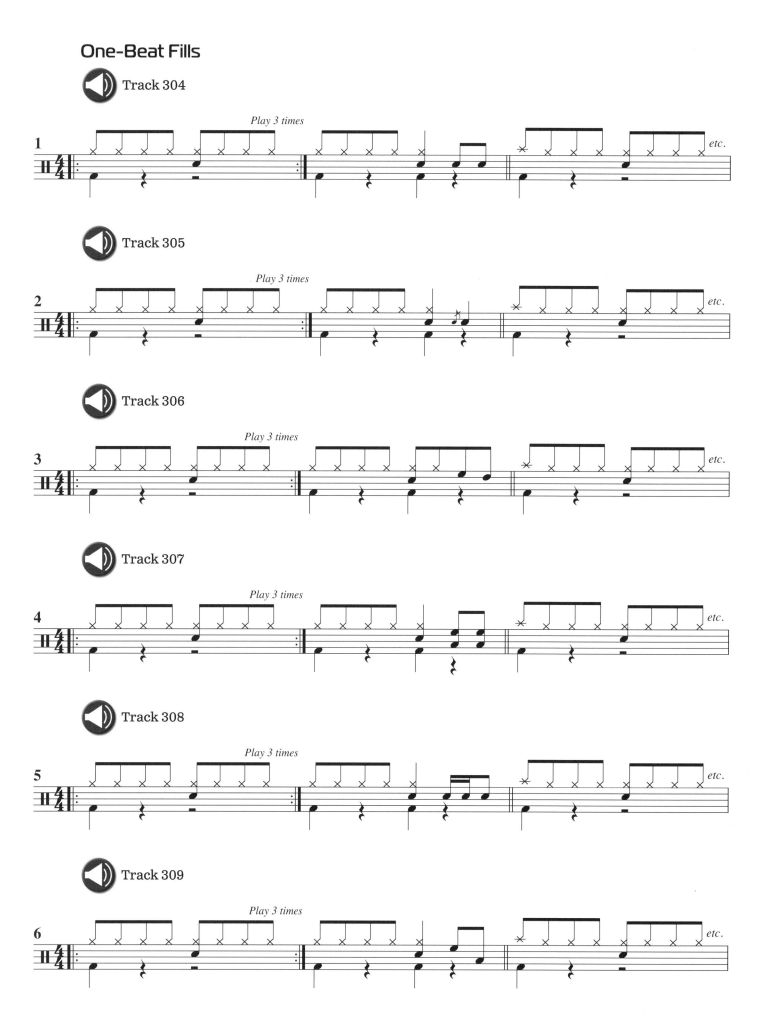

Track 305

Track 306

Track 307

Track 308

Track 309

# TWO-STEP BEATS

Another groove you will find in rock music is the *two-step*. This type of beat is found often in country, bluegrass, and folk music. It's one of the simplest and most enjoyable to play. We'll write this beat as an eighth-note beat in 2/4. Because it's simple and direct, there will be fewer variations, and we'll write these all as two-bar patterns.

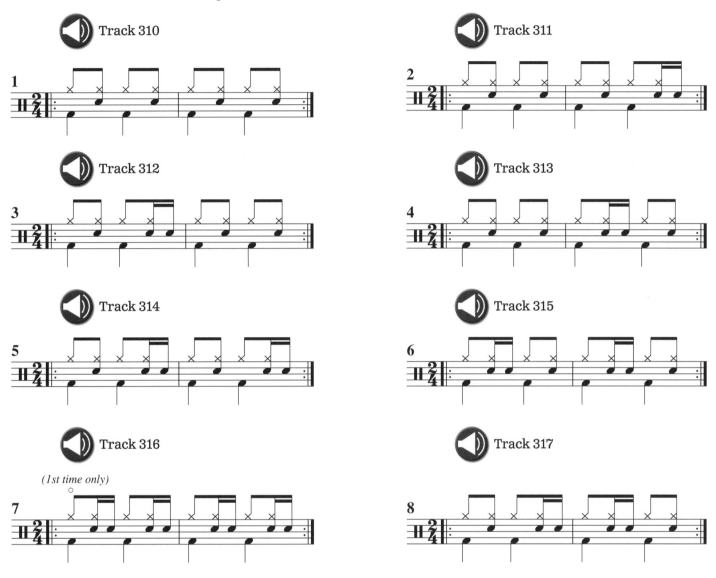

A two-step can also be played as sixteenth notes on the snare drum, with accents on the "and" counts. This is more common in bluegrass and country music, and it can be played with sticks or brushes depending on the nature of the tune.

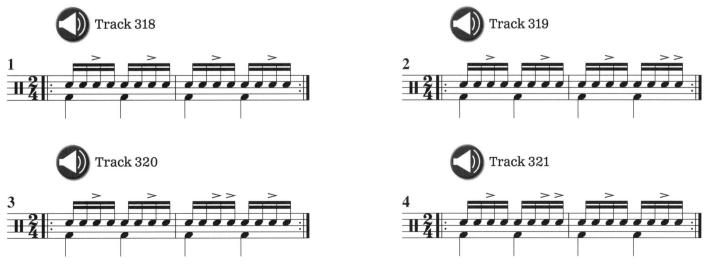

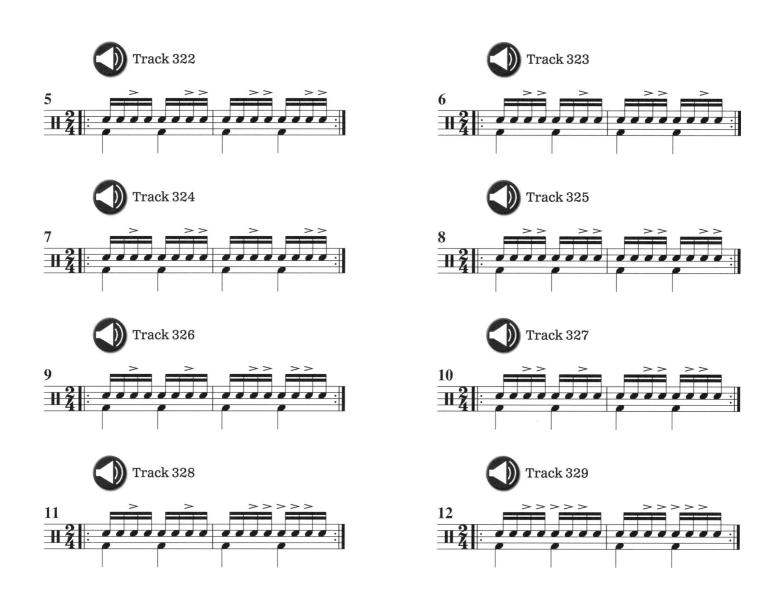

# TWO-STEP BEATS WITH FILLS

For this section, and because the two-step is written in 2/4, we'll use an "eight-bar phrase with a two-bar fill" concept. This is the same the "four-bar phrase with a fill" concept for beats written in 4/4.

## Two-Bar Fills

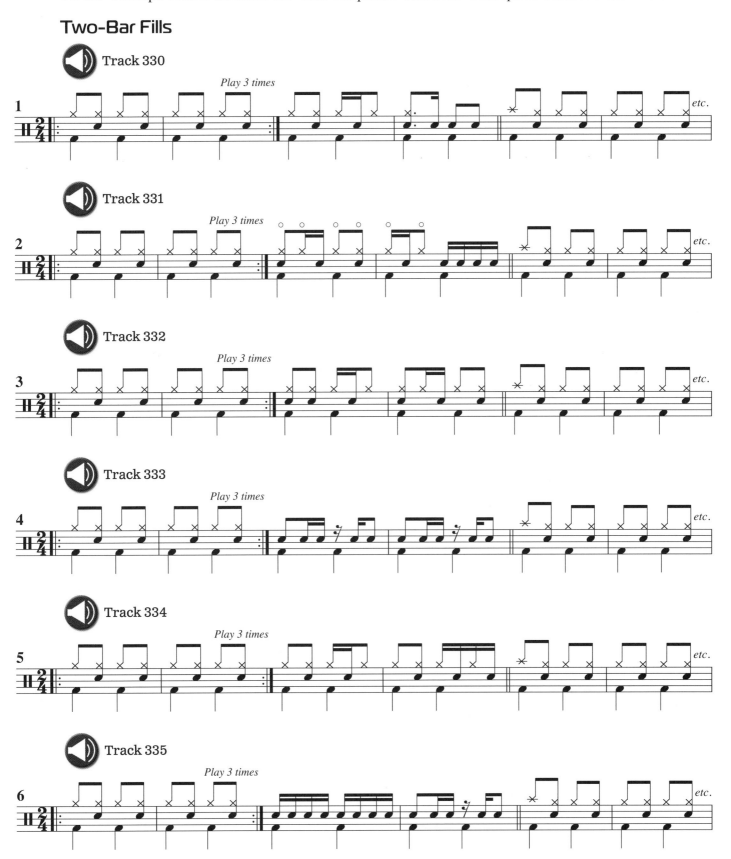

## One-Bar Fills

These are eight-bar phrases with the fill occurring in the last bar (in 2/4) of the phrase.

Track 336

Track 337

Track 338

Track 339

Track 340

Track 341

# DOUBLE TIME BEATS

Another cool groove found in rock is the *double time beat*. This is similar to the two-step in that the snare is on the "backbeat," which, in a two-step is the "and" of the "1" and "2" counts.

 Track 342

In a double time beat, which will be written here in "cut time"—or a quarter note feel in 4/4—the snare is on beat 2 and 4, and the tempo is fast.

 Track 343

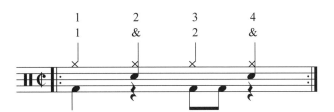

The difference between the two-step and the double time beats is in the bass drum; the bass drum tends to be more syncopated in the double time feel. That being said, for our purposes here, the bass drum will always play on beat 1.

Here are some double time beats that you'll find useful. Once mastered at a slower tempo, these beats should be played fast! Try them at ♩ = 200 bpm or faster!

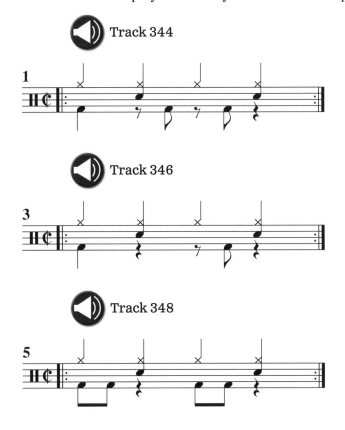

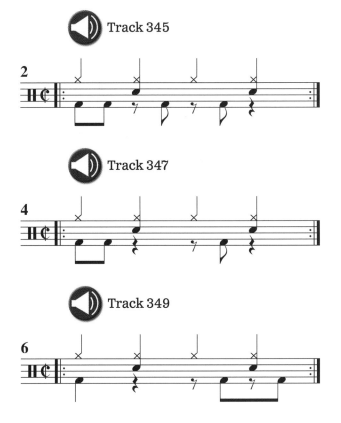

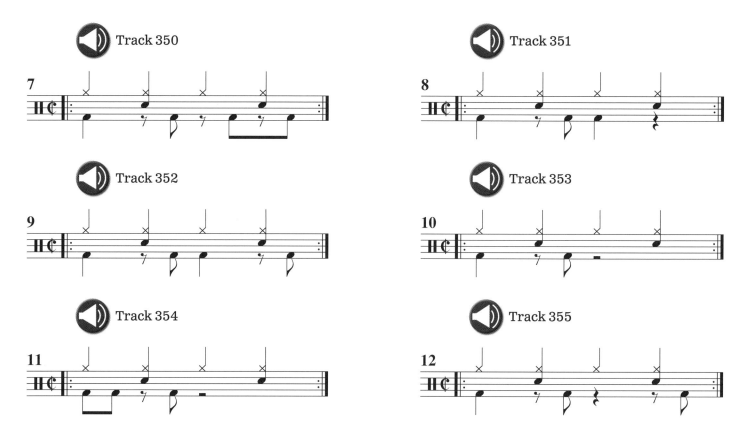

Now let's check out some common two-bar double time beats that rockers often use. Again, master them at a slow tempo, but then crank up the tempo to ♩ = 200 bmp or faster!

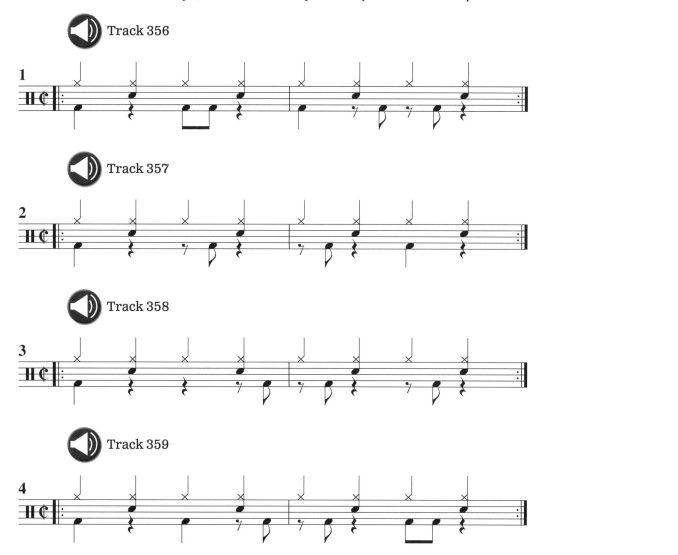

Track 360

Track 361

Track 362

Track 363

# DOUBLE TIME BEATS WITH FILLS

As with the two-step beats, we'll use an "eight-bar phrase with a two-bar fill" to explore fills for double time beats. We'll use a two-bar double time beat as our basis here.

## Two-Bar Fills

Track 364

Track 365

Track 366

Track 367

Track 368

Track 369

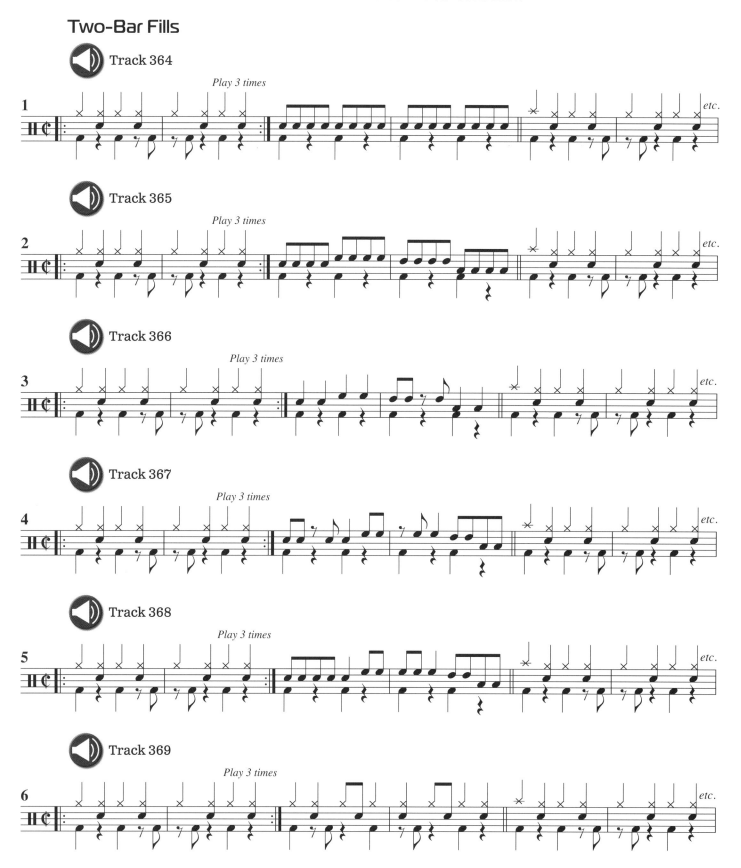

## Two-Beat Fills

This is the same idea as the previous section, but we'll use a two-beat fill in the eighth bar of the phrase on beats 3 and 4.

**Track 370**

**Track 371**

**Track 372**

**Track 373**

**Track 374**

**Track 375**

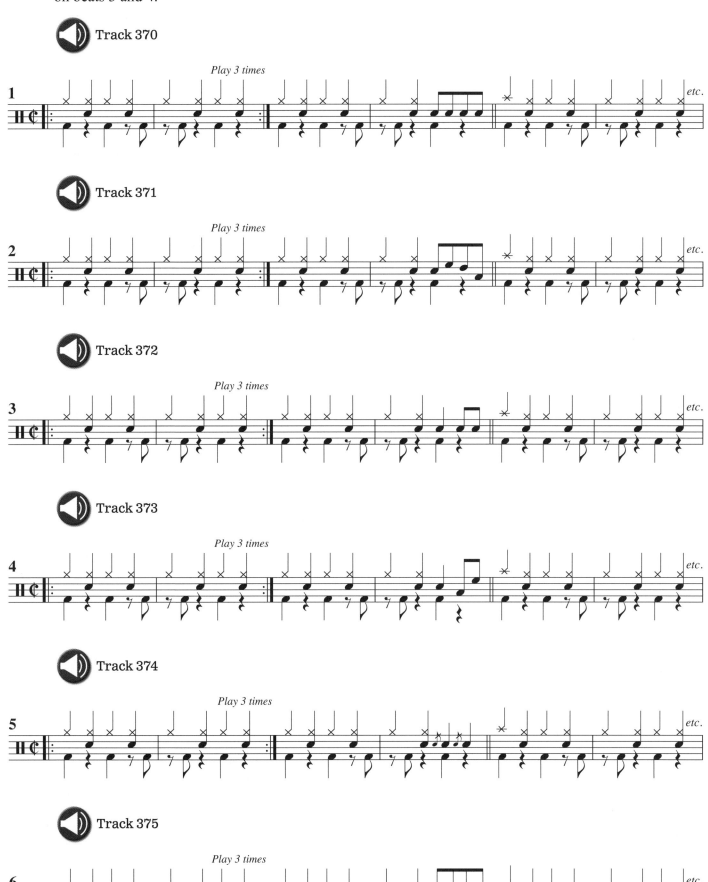

# BEATS WITH QUARTER NOTES ON THE SNARE

Although not overly common, grooves with the snare drum on the quarter notes can be very powerful and create a muscular, driving rock beat.

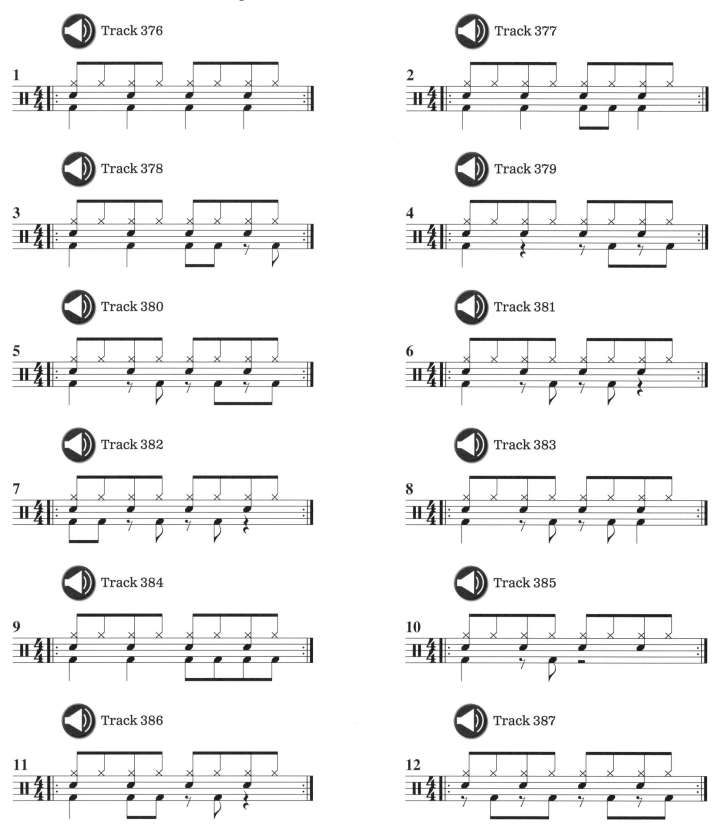

# OTHER COOL GROOVES

## Rock Ballads

Often, beats like these are used in slower ballads. They give a lot of space to the music, allowing for the vocals, guitar, and keyboards to soar.

Track 388

Track 389

Track 390

Track 391

Track 392

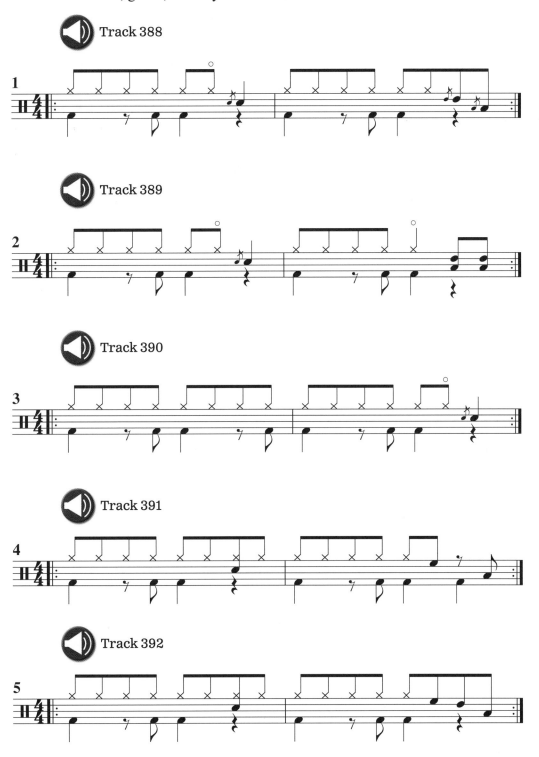

## Surf Beats

Surf music is a classic style of rock that came out of the surf culture of the fifties and sixties. This type of beat is usually played at a quick tempo. All of these beats can be played on the ride cymbal or the hi-hat.

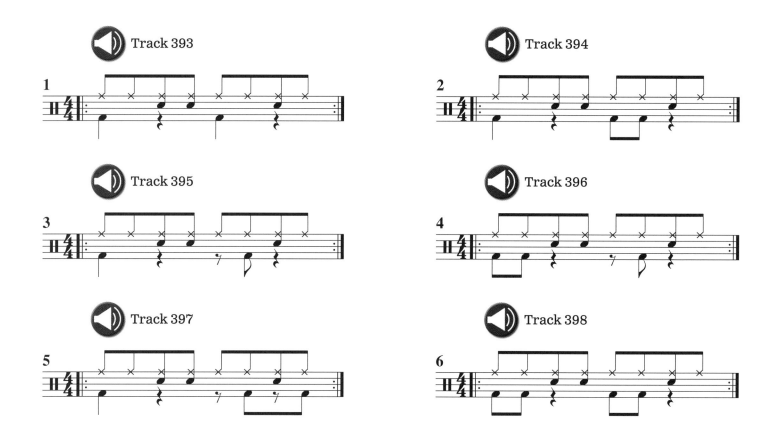

## Latin Rock

Latin rock is yet another hybrid style that integrates some Afro-Cuban elements into the rock feel by using the toms and snare in a way similar to conga rhythms.

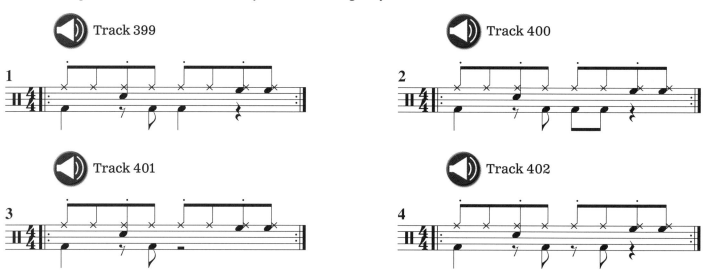

## The Dance Beat

This is a variation of the first beat in the book that's used in rock and in dance music.

# THE COUNT OFFS

So now that you've learned all these great beats and fills, and you have the ammunition and knowledge to play with a rock band, let's learn how to count them off properly.

## Eighth-Note Classic Rock Beats

Use stick clicks and count.

🔊 Track 404

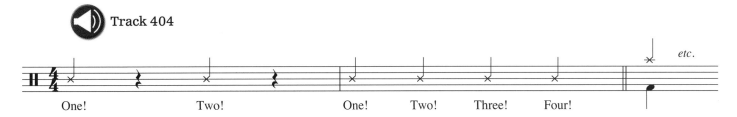

One!      Two!      One!    Two!    Three!    Four!

You can also kick the band in by adding a snare hit on the fourth beat of the second bar of the count off.

🔊 Track 405

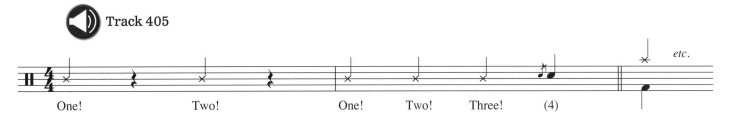

One!      Two!      One!    Two!    Three!    (4)

Or this next one is cool too:

🔊 Track 406

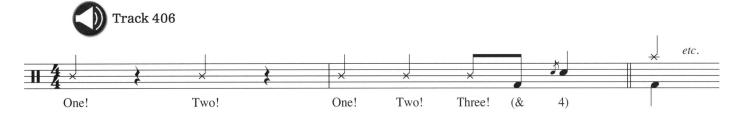

One!      Two!      One!    Two!    Three!   (&    4)

## Classic R&B

🔊 Track 407

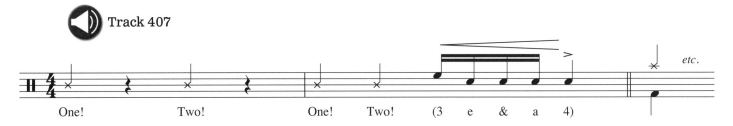

One!      Two!      One!    Two!    (3   e   &   a   4)

## Quarter-Note Classic Rock Beats

🔊 Track 408

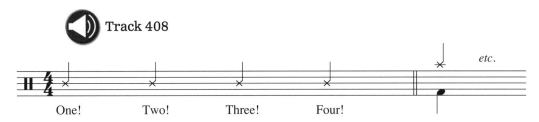

One!    Two!    Three!    Four!

Or this one works as well:

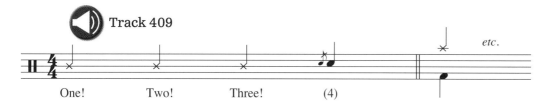

Track 409

One!     Two!     Three!     (4)     *etc.*

## Funky Rock Beats

For moderate tempo funky rock beats, this works well:

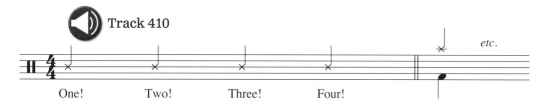

Track 410

One!     Two!     Three!     Four!     *etc.*

Or try this one:

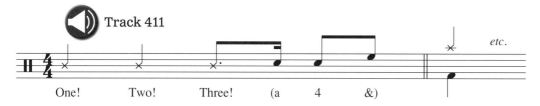

Track 411

One!     Two!     Three!     (a    4    &)     *etc.*

## Rock Shuffle Beats

A four quarter-note stick click will work for a shuffle, but you could also use the following:

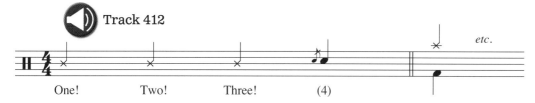

Track 412

One!     Two!     Three!     (4)     *etc.*

Or this one is nice as well:

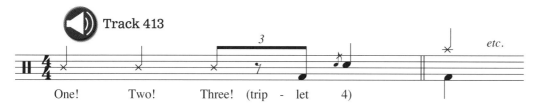

Track 413

One!     Two!     Three! (trip - let   4)     *etc.*

## 12/8 Beats

Click the twelve counts while saying "1, 2, 3, 4" on the dotted-quarter-note pulse of the 12/8 measure.

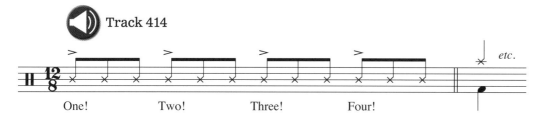

Track 414

One!     Two!     Three!     Four!     *etc.*

Here's another one.

**Track 415**

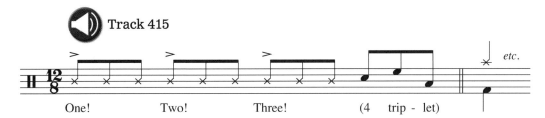

One!　　　Two!　　　Three!　　　(4　trip - let)　　*etc.*

## Half Time Beats

**Track 416**

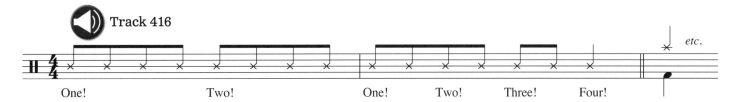

One!　　　　　Two!　　　　One!　　Two!　　Three!　Four!　　*etc.*

Or this works well too:

**Track 417**

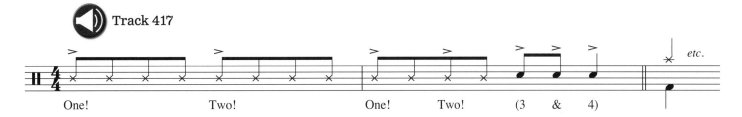

One!　　　　　Two!　　　　One!　　Two!　　(3　&　4)　　*etc.*

## Two-Step Beats

**Track 418**

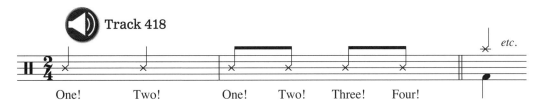

One!　　　Two!　　　One!　Two!　Three!　Four!　　*etc.*

## Double Time Beats

The two-step count off works for a double time tune as well, only we write it in cut time. But it will sound the same as the two-step count off:

**Track 419**

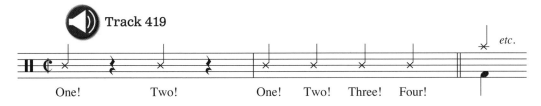

One!　　　　Two!　　　One!　Two!　Three!　Four!　　*etc.*

## Beats with Quarter Notes on the Snare

This also works for a dance beat.

**Track 420**

One!　　　Two!　　　Three!　　And!　　Four!　　*etc.*

## Latin Rock

For a mid-tempo Latin rock tune, you can use a straight quarter-note count off:

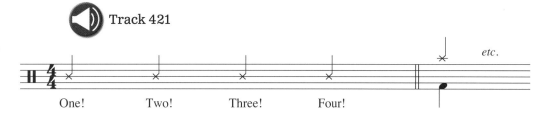

Track 421

Or try this one:

Track 422

## Surf Beats

Track 423

## Rock Ballads

Track 424

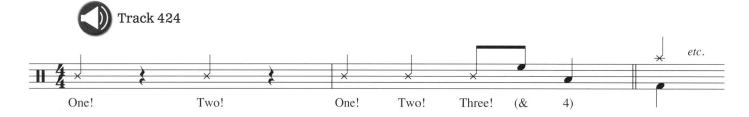

OK! So you know a whole bunch of grooves, fills, and count offs in the rock 'n' roll style. Now let's play some rock 'n' roll!!! Ready?

Track 425

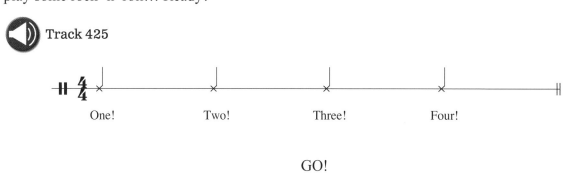

GO!